BIG Earth Facts

BIG EARTH FACTS PICTURE CREDITS

P4 Pictor International, p5 Corbis, p6 t PJ Devries Oxford Scientific Films, c Flip Chalfant Getty Images, b Lieve Verschuier Bridgeman Art Library, p7 tr Pauline Cutler Getty Images, p8 Corbis Stockmarket, p 9 t & c Corbis Stockmarket, b Kevin Schafer NHPA, p10 t Louisjoy Thurston Bubbles, p 10-11 & b Corbis Stockmarket, p12 cl & cr Natural History Museum Picture Library, p14 c Gary Yeowell Getty Images, p16 bl Daniel Heuclin NHPA, cr Pictor International, p 17 t Daryl Balfour NHPA, b Francois Gohier Ardea, 16-17 Andre Gallant Getty Images, p18 b GK & Vicki Hart, t Rodger Jackman Oxford Scientific Films, p19 Hugh Sitton Getty Images, 20 bl Pictor International, cr Hans Peter Merten Bruce Coleman Collection, tr Paul Chesley Getty Images, p21 Pictor International, p23 David Cayless Oxford Scientific Films, p24 Image State, p25 Gabor Geissler Getty Images, p27 tl Bob Gibbons Ardea, tr Jules Cowan Bruce Coleman Collection, p29 tl Robert Holland Getty Images, tr Brian & Cherry Alexander NHPA, b John Mason Ardea, p30 Mark Jones Oxford Scientific Films, p30-31 b Jean Paul Ferrero Ardea, 30-31 Michael Melford Getty Images, p32-33 Jeff Hunter Getty Images, p 33 t Staffan Widstrand Bruce Coleman Collection, p34 Joseph Van O's Getty Images, p35 tr Nigel Dennis NHPA, bc Martin harvey NHPA, l Ferrero-Labat Ardea, p36 Pictor International, p37 tl Mike Slater Oxford Scientific Films, tr Daniel Heuclin NHPA, c Pictor Internatinal, bl Heather Angel Natural Visions, p38 cr & c Nick Gordon Ardea, p39 tr Britstock IFA, bl Haroldo Palo Jr NHPA, p40 Pictor International, 41 tl John Shaw NHPA, tr Peter Gould Oxford Scientific Films, br John Daniels Ardea, p41 tr Image State, p43 tr Claude Nuridsany & Marie Perennou Science Photo Library, b Pictor International, p44 Craig Hamman Corbis Stockmarket, p45 tr Pascal Goetgheluck Ardea, p49 tl Stephen Dalton FLPA, cr Corbis Stockmarket, bl David Woodfall NHPA, p50 t Pictor International, bl Peter Cade Getty Images, br Daniel Heuclin NHPA, p 51 cr Daniel Heuclin NHPA, p52 tl Pictor International, br Francis Lepine Oxford Scientific Films, p53 t Terje Rakke Getty Images, b Ian West Bubbles p54 bl Andre Gallant Getty Images, tr Corbis Stockmarket, p55 tl & bc Pictor International, cr Richard Packwood Oxford Scientific Films, p56 t Ake Lindau Ardea, b Oxford Scientific Films, p57 l Galen Rowell Corbis, br E Mickleburgh Ardea, P58 cl James Davis Getty Images, tr Mark Dadswell All Sport, bc Stephen Dalton NHPA, p60 bc & cl Pictor International, tr Philippe Gelot Getty Images, p61 tr Corbis Stockmarket, cr Getty Images, bl A Foley Getty Images, p62 Stephen Dalton NHPA, p63 tl Ian Beames Ardea, bl Melvin Grey NHPA, br GI Bernard NHPA, p64 l J Bottomly Ardea, cr Laura Campbell NHPA, br Chris Knights Ardea, p65 br Roger Wilmshurst FLPA, tr Chris Martin Bahr Ardea, p66 & 67 Corbis Stockmarket, p67 tr EA Janes NHPA, p68 l Loisjoy Thurston Bubbles, tr Brian Shuel Collections, p69 tl Britstock-IFA, cr David Woodfall NHPA, p70 tr Stephen Dalton NHPA, cl Chris Knights Ardea, cr Bob Gibbons Ardea, p71 tr Ingo Arndt Bruce Coleman Collection, bl Gary Higgins DK Images, p72 tr FLPA, b Corbis Stockmarket, p73 l Richard Packwood Oxford Scientific Films, r Ian Royd Getty Images, p74 bl Corbis Stockmarket, tr Heather Angel Natural Visions, p75 tl & cr Heather Angel Natural Visions, bl M Watson Ardea, p76 t Wolfgang Wagner Ardea, c FLPA, p77 tr Roger Wilmshurst FLPA, b Werner Zepf NHPA, p79 c L Batten FLPA, tr Bruce Coleman Collection, br Martin Bond Science Photo Library

Published by Armadillo Books
An imprint of Bookmart Limited
Registered Number 2372865
Trading as Bookmart Limited
Desford Road
Enderby
Leicester
LE9 5AD

ISBN 1843220482

Produced for Bookmart by Planet Three Publishing Network,
10 Northburgh Street, London EC1V 0AT.

PLANET THREE PUBLISHING NETWORK

Printed in Singapore

BIG Earth Facts

ARMADILLO

Contents

Fire

Good and bad

Blazing log fires and flickering candles make our homes cosy. But when a fire gets out of control, it is dangerous. Whether it's good or bad, fire is an important part of life.

Bad for the planet

Lots of rainforest is burned each year so that the land can be cleared for farming.

This harms our planet because the trees are not replanted, rare plants die and lots of animals lose their homes.

The Great Fire of London

In 1666, a small fire started in London's Pudding Lane. The fire quickly spread through the city and lasted for several days.
It destroyed thousands of homes and churches.

Festive fire

All over the world, people use fire to light up their annual festivals and celebrations.

On Bonfire Nights, New Year's Eves and Saints' days, adults light fires and fireworks and children play with sparklers.

Fires and fireworks also mark special occasions, like parades and competitions.

Flames of life

On your birthday, your cake has one lit candle to mark each year of your life. And at the Olympics, a special flame is lit to open the world's biggest games.

Volcanoes

Nature's fireworks
Volcanoes are huge, fiery mountains. Hot melted rock and scorching gases force their way up to the surface from deep underground. When a volcano erupts, fire and flames spurt out of the top like a great firework. Beware, volcanoes are very dangerous!

New explosions!

This volcano was dormant. Here it has erupted again through cracks in the side of the mountain.

Geysers

These are fountains of boiling water which form when water trapped underground is heated up by hot rocks.

Steam forms too, and the steam and boiling water then burst out of the ground in a jet.

Liquid fire

"Lava" is the red-hot rock that explodes out of a volcano. It is so hot that it melts and turns into liquid. Lava pours over the land, destroying everything in its path.

Rocks

What is rock?

Our planet is made up of lots of different types of rock. The rock inside the Earth is very hot and some of it has melted into a liquid. But the Earth's surface or "crust", which we walk around on, is cold and hard.

The Giant's Causeway

The Giant's Causeway in Northern Ireland is a strange rock formation.

The story goes that a giant built it as a path across the sea to Scotland. In fact, it was formed when a lava lake dried up.

Diamonds

Diamonds are the hardest of all rocks. They make beautiful jewellery and, because they are so hard, they can be used to cut glass.

Rocks at home

What use is a lump of rock?
Rocks are often ground up, heated or mixed with other ingredients to make the things we find in our homes. Some rocks used in houses, like marble and slate, look the same as they do in the ground.

Look around. Which rocks can you find in your home?

Galena is a type of lead used to hold stained glass windows together.

Marble is often used to make statues, work surfaces and floor tiles.

Haematite is used to make iron railings, fences and gates.

Quartz batteries are used for watches, clocks and timers.

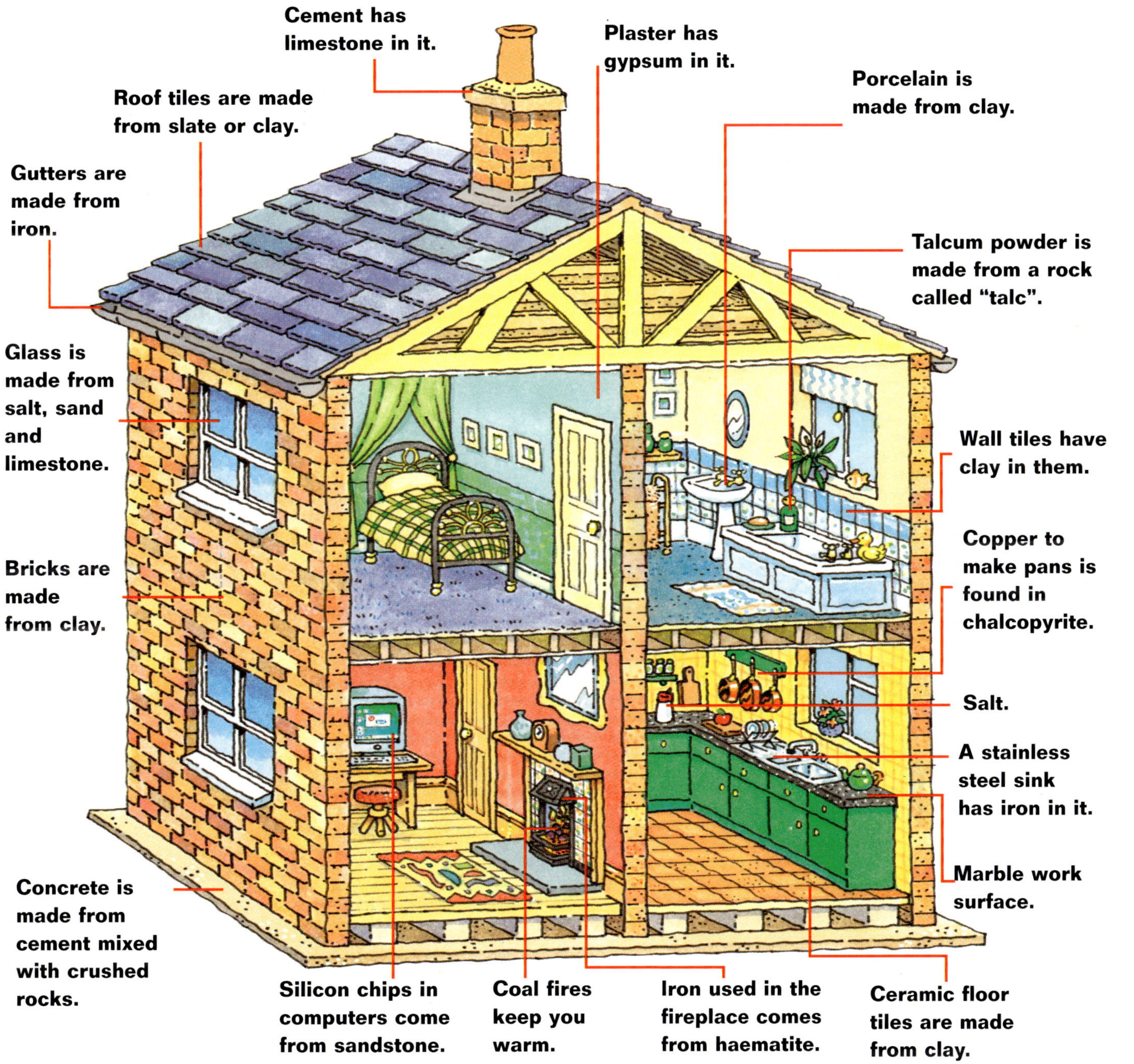
Cement has limestone in it.
Plaster has gypsum in it.
Roof tiles are made from slate or clay.
Porcelain is made from clay.
Gutters are made from iron.
Talcum powder is made from a rock called "talc".
Glass is made from salt, sand and limestone.
Wall tiles have clay in them.
Copper to make pans is found in chalcopyrite.
Bricks are made from clay.
Salt.
A stainless steel sink has iron in it.
Marble work surface.
Concrete is made from cement mixed with crushed rocks.
Silicon chips in computers come from sandstone.
Coal fires keep you warm.
Iron used in the fireplace comes from haematite.
Ceramic floor tiles are made from clay.

Mountainside

Wild and rugged homes

Mountains are cold places where only the toughest creatures live. The plants are few and hardy, and the animals are wild and avoid human contact.

Changing seasons

In winter, snow covers the mountains and many animals shelter in the valleys below.

Then, when spring arrives and plants begin to grow again on the mountainside, animals and birds return to feed and have babies.

The peregrine falcon can fly as fast as an antelope can run.

This ptarmigan has its summer feathers. In the autumn, it turns white to hide in the snow.

The wild cat looks like a big pet cat, but it is a wild animal and does not like people.

Gorse and heather grow on mountains, where the wind and poor soil make it hard for other plants to grow.

Some goats that used to be tame have returned to the wild and are called “feral”.

The golden eagle is a bird of prey which means that it hunts small animals.

Ravens look like giant crows. They live in the mountains and other high areas.

This mountain hare is in its summer coat. In winter, it turns white.

The desert

Mountains of sand

The largest desert in the world is the Sahara, in Africa. It's a huge place, about the same size as the USA!

In the Sahara desert, strong winds whip the sand into hills as high as a skyscraper, and over five kilometres wide! These sand mountains shift and change shape whenever the wind blows. Over the years, they have blown over and hidden whole towns and ancient cities.

Desert people

Bedouin people have lived in the Sahara, Syrian and Arabian deserts for thousands of years. They live together in large tents and travel across the deserts with their camels and goats.

Oasis

An oasis is a pool of fresh water in a desert. Plants grow around the water, animals stop to drink and people sometimes live there.

Clever plants

Not many plants grow in dry, desert conditions. The ones that do have special ways of saving water. This saguaro cactus, the largest in the world, stores water inside its stem. Its prickles protect it from animals who try to eat it.

Desert life

Hot, hot, hot!

Phew! It's hot in the desert. In fact, deserts are the hottest places on Earth. So the animals and plants that live there have found clever ways to survive. Let's find out more...

Hide-and-sleep!

To escape from the sun, gerbils dig burrows in the sand. They keep the burrow cool by blocking the hole with sand so that hot air can't get in.

When it's cool at night, they come out to search for food.

Thirsty work

Desert geckos scurry across the sand quickly, hunting insects. The insects' blood provides geckos with water so that they don't need to drink.

Sand survivors

Camels can walk through a desert for days without eating or drinking anything.

Before a long journey, a camel will eat and drink lots. This food and water turns to fat and is stored in its humps. The camel lives on the fat when there's nothing else to eat.

Australian outback

What is the outback?

Australia has miles of hot, dry countryside called the "outback". It would take days to drive across it. If you did, you'd see some amazing animals.

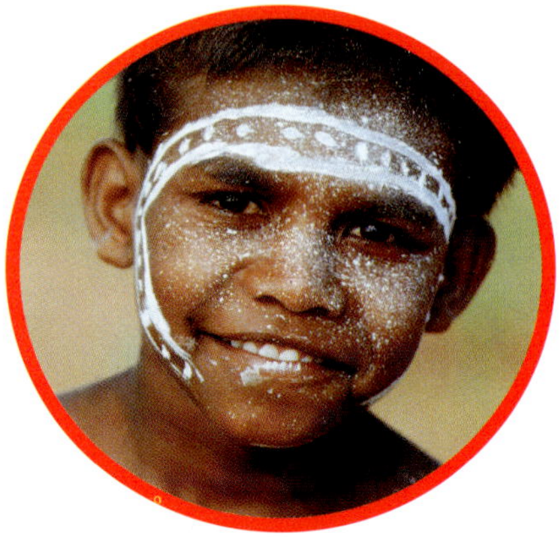

Hop along

Animals called "marsupials" live in Australia. They carry their babies in a body pouch. A mother kangaroo carries her baby "joey" for a year.

At home

Aboriginal people belong to the race that first lived in Australia.

Uluru

Uluru is a "monolith": a giant, single rock. It is made of red sandstone but the colour seems to change throughout the day.

Cute koalas!

Koalas are marsupials too. These small, tailless animals spend their time in eucalyptus trees all over Australia. They move slowly, eating the leaves.

Koalas are timid and gentle. They have large, leathery noses and fluffy ears.

The seaside

At the beach

The beach is a wonderful place to be on a summer's day. It's fun to explore the seashore, paddle, eat ice cream and wander down the pier.

Driftwood boat

Look for a chunky bit of driftwood to make a boat and a thin piece for the mast. To make a sail, glue fabric to card and cut out a triangle. Glue it to the mast. Ask an adult to bore a hole into the centre of the boat. Squeeze glue into the hole and stick the mast into it.

Beachcombing

"Beachcombing" means searching for interesting things on the beach.

Look for driftwood, seaweed, starfish and crabs along the "high tide line". This is the point the waves reach when it is high tide. Waves leave behind lots of things from the sea.

Rock pools

Rock pools are good places to find treasures such as crabs and fish. Remember to put them back in the same place.

Bird watching

If you like watching birds, beaches are great places to see seabirds of all kinds, from the common seagull (above) to kittiwakes, skewers and gannets. Watch how they fight, feed and play. If you find any nests, keep your distance so that you don't scare the birds away.

Harbours

What is a harbour?

A harbour is a safe area of coast where boats can shelter from the sea.

Fishermen bring their boats into the harbour, loaded with fish. The fish are taken to the local market and sold.

Not for swimming!

In olden days, people learned to swim in sheltered harbours or in ponds. Today, we have swimming pools and other places to help us. Now it's dangerous to swim among the harbour boats.

Harbour walls have thick posts called "stanchions" near their edge. Boats tie up to them with strong ropes.

Tyres hang down from harbour walls to stop boats from hitting the stones.

Tankers carry oil across the world. They are some of the largest ships ever built.

Lifebelts

You may see a red and white ring like this by the sea. It is a "lifebelt". It can be thrown to anyone who has fallen into the sea, to help them float and to pull them to safety.

Beaches

Where do beaches come from?

Beaches are built by waves. When big waves crash against cliffs, they break off chunks of rock. The chunks break up into pebbles or sand in the sea. In sheltered areas, the waves wash the sand or pebbles back onto the shore, making a beach.

Wave power!

Waves are so strong they can break up cliffs. This archway was made by waves crashing against the rocks.

Sea art

Bits of wood that fall into the sea also get shaped and smoothed by the waves. This is called "driftwood". Look out for driftwood that has been washed onto the beach.

Where do waves come from?

Waves are made by the wind far out at sea. Then they are blown towards land.

When a wave gets near a beach, the sea is not deep enough for the wave to keep going, so it slows down at the bottom, rolls over at the top, and breaks onto the shore.

Wind

What is it?

Wind is air moving from one place to another.

Scattered seeds

Some plants use the wind to carry their seeds to new ground.

Have you ever wondered where the wind comes from?

When the sun shines, it heats up the ground and the air just above it.

This warm air is lighter than cold air, so it starts to rise.

As the warm air goes up, cold air rushes in to take its place. That's wind!

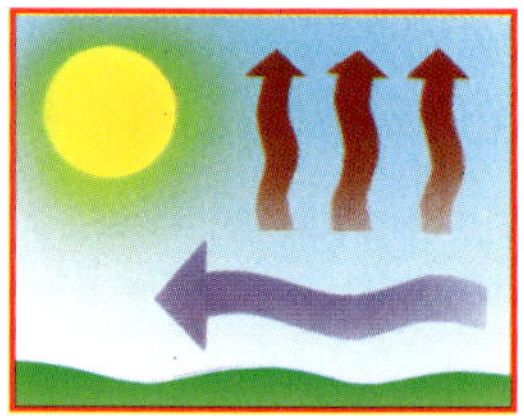

Biting winds
The world's windiest place is around the South Pole. Fierce winds speed over the icy land. They are so strong they could knock a tree over.

It's a breeze!

Wind can be fun. Watch out for windsurfers and yachts when you are at the seaside.

Windy signs

The wind is invisible. But you can feel and see when the wind is blowing. Look out for trees and leaves blowing around.

Islands

What is an island?

An island is a piece of land surrounded by water. There are tiny desert islands where nobody lives and far-distant islands full of strange wildlife or signs of early people. Let's go and explore.

Strange creatures

There are lots of animals and birds living on the Galapagos Islands. These creatures are not found anywhere else in the world. They include giant tortoises that can live for up to 150 years!

Coral islands

Coral islands are low, flat islands set in tropical seas. The land is made up of tiny pieces of coral which have been ground up and pushed together by the sea.

Easter Island

Easter Island is one of the most faraway islands in the world. It is famous for the giant carved stones that stand around the edge.

The first European landed there on Easter Day in 1722 and called it Easter Island.

Coral reefs

Reef life

Coral reefs are full of surprises. They look like fantastic underwater rock gardens, and are home to millions of tiny animals and colourful plants.

What are they?

Coral reefs look like colourful, spiky rocks but, in fact, they are made up of lots of tiny animals that live together, forming amazing shapes.

Coral reefs are found on the seabed in warm, shallow seas.

Take the plunge

Some coral reefs are found just below the surface of the water. People swimming with a mask and snorkel can explore the beautiful coral.

Fishy heaven

Many beautiful creatures, including turtles and colourful fish, swim in the warm waters around coral reefs. They hide in the coral and find food there.

On safari

Africa's animals

Africa is home to some of the most amazing animals in the world. Let's go on an African safari adventure to meet some of these wonderful creatures...

King lion

Just look at those teeth! Lions live in groups called "prides". During the day, the whole pride rests together in the shade. They wait until the sun goes down before hunting for food.

The females do most of the hunting, but the males eat the most!

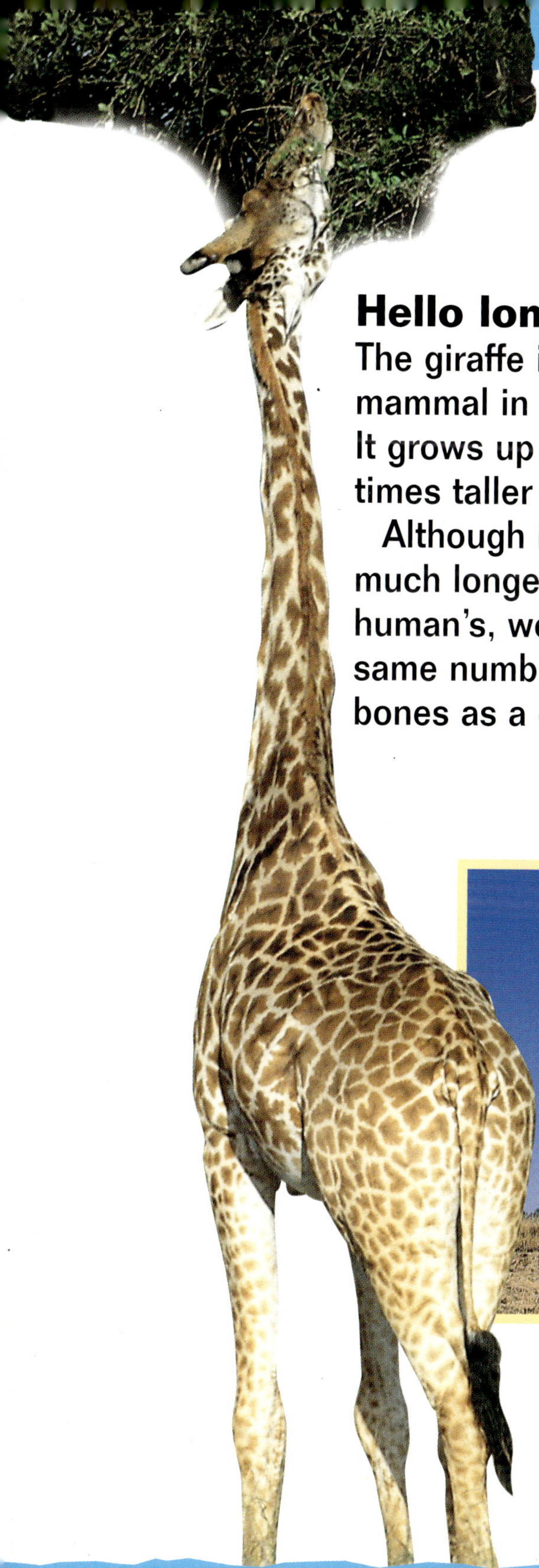

Hello long neck!

The giraffe is the tallest mammal in the world. It grows up to three times taller than a man.

Although its neck is much longer than a human's, we have the same number of neck bones as a giraffe!

African elephant

The African elephant is the largest land mammal on Earth. It is as tall as two men and weighs as much as 80 humans!

Charge!

The black rhinoceros is huge, with leathery skin and two big horns. Although it's heavy, it can run fast.

The black rhino has bad eyesight but a good sense of smell and excellent hearing.

Man-made forests

Why plant forests?

Many forests are specially planted to grow trees for wood.

The wood, or "timber", is used to make furniture, toys or paper and waxes and oils too. So wood is very useful!

Timber!

People who cut down trees in forests are called "lumberjacks". They use powerful saws to cut down the trees.

Food trees
Some trees are planted for their fruit too. Even the bark and sap can be used to make treats!

Chocolate trees
Chocolate is made from the beans of the cocoa tree. The beans grow inside pods.

Sweet trees
Maple syrup comes from the sap, or juice, of the sugar maple tree. Tubes are pushed into the tree and the sap drips into a collecting bucket.

Spicy trees
The cooking spice, cinnamon, comes from the bark of a tree.

Quick harvest

Pine trees are often planted in man-made forests because they grow quickly.

Heave!

Imagine lifting a tree! When trees are chopped down, they are very heavy. So they are either carried by trucks, or floated along rivers, to the sawmills to be cut into logs.

The logs are taken to paper mills or factories where they are made into new products.

Rainforests

Hot and rainy world

Rainforests are found around the centre of the Earth, near the Equator. Here, the sun shines almost every day and it's very hot. It rains a lot too. In the Amazon rainforest it pours with rain almost every day.

Forest home

This little girl is a Yanomami. The Yanomami people have lived in the Amazon forests for thousands of years.

Night hunter

The jaguar is the largest cat in the Amazon. It sleeps in trees during the day and hunts at night.

Fab fact!

Did you know that the Amazon rainforest is home to more kinds of animals and plants than anywhere else in the world?

Weird and wonderful

Colourful birds like the toucan live high up in the treetops. This part of the rainforest is called the "canopy". Toucans eat berries and fruit that grow on the trees.

Clouds

Look up!

White and fluffy or black and thundery, clouds are amazing things! There are lots of different kinds of cloud, so look up and see which ones you can spot as they float by. Can you see shapes in them?

What are clouds?

Clouds are made up of millions of small droplets of water, or tiny pieces of ice. Rain falls when the droplets, or bits of ice, become too big and heavy to stay in the sky.

Cloud-spotting

There are special names for different kinds of clouds.

Cumulus

Cumulus clouds are large, fluffy clouds that look like puffs of cotton wool. Cumulus means "heap".

Nimbus

Nimbus means "rain". Nimbus clouds are dark grey rain-clouds. They also make thunder and lightning.

Cirrus

Cirrus clouds are high and wispy and made of ice. Cirrus means "curl of hair".

Rain

Wet, wet, wet!

"Oh no, it's raining!" How many times have you said that? But rain is very important. Every plant and animal on Earth needs rain to help it survive.

How is rain made?

Warm, wet air rises up into the sky from the sea. As it rises, the warm air cools and turns into tiny water droplets which form clouds. Cold air high in the sky changes clouds back to water so that it falls back down as rain.

Measure the rain

Why not make your own rain gauge to measure how much rain falls each day?

On a clear container, use a ruler and marker pen to mark off 15 centimetres. Put the container outside. When it has rained, check to see how much rain fell.

Fun and rain

Some countries get plenty of rain and everybody moans about it. But some places, like parts of the Atacama Desert in Chile, have not had rain for 400 years!

So next time you get a shower of rain, put on your mac and wellies, run outside and enjoy it!

Hailstones

Cold air turns clouds into heavy drops of rain. But very cold air makes the drops freeze. These fall to Earth as hailstones, which are usually small ice balls. The biggest hailstone ever seen was bigger than a football!

Rainbows

Making rainbows

Sunlight is made up of lots of colours mixed together. Rainbows occur when the sun shines through drops of rain. That's because when sun shines through water droplets, the light breaks up into all its different colours, making a rainbow.

Full circle

Rainbows are really circles, not arcs. But we can't see the whole circle because the Earth blocks our view of it.

If the sun is low in the sky, you can see much more of the rainbow. But if you travel in a plane, you can sometimes see a whole rainbow!

Colourful bugs

Some insects have bodies or wings that reflect rainbow colours. Scientists call them "iridescent". Look out for rainbow colours on dragonflies, beetles and butterfly wings.

The colours of the rainbow are:

- Red
- Orange
- Yellow
- Green
- Blue
- Indigo
- Violet

Bogs

Dragonflies buzz over marshes looking for smaller flying insects to eat. They lay their eggs in bogs or shallow water.

What is a bog?

A bog is a place where the ground is soft and squishy because the soil is soaked with water.

Trees can't grow here because the ground is so soft that they would fall over. Only special plants, which like damp or wet soil, live here.

The marsh fritillary butterfly is often seen near bogs. Its caterpillars hide under silky webs.

The spotted crake is shy and stays hidden. You are more likely to hear one than see it. Its call sounds like a whip crack!

The sundew is a very strange bog plant! It eats flies and other insects that become trapped on its sticky stems.

The yellow wagtail eats flying insects. It was given its name because it is yellow and wags its tail up and down as it walks along!

Midges are tiny insects that fly around in big clouds. Some bite but they make good food for birds and other insects.

The frog is the most common bogland animal. Frogs often catch flying insects by flicking out their long, sticky tongues.

Grass snakes are usually found in boggy areas near water and they're very good swimmers! They eat frogs, tadpoles and fish.

Rivers

Bank life

Have you noticed that lots of plants grow close to rivers and streams? This is because they have lots to drink here.

These plants make good hiding places for land animals such as rats and water voles. Fish also hide between the roots and under the overhanging leaves.

Measuring floods

The water levels in rivers and lakes rises when it rains a lot. After a flood, when the water has gone down, you may see lines on the tree trunks. These lines show how high the water reached.

The biggest river

The River Amazon carries more water than any other river in the world. At some places, the Amazon is too wide for a person on one bank to see the other side.

Wonderful willows

The weeping willow is the easiest tree to spot beside ponds and rivers. Its drooping branches hang down and its leaves often trail in the water. Willow twigs are bendy and are used to make baskets.

Water

Turn on the tap

The water that comes out of the tap in your kitchen sink is clean and safe to drink.

When water goes down the drain, it's pumped away to a special place to be cleaned. Here, the dirt and germs are taken out of the water. It is then pumped back into people's homes and used all over again!

Pure water

We are lucky to have clean water to drink. Some people in other countries become ill because their water is dirty.

Flood thirst

Floods can even cause water shortages! This happens when muddy flood water leaks into wells and water pipes. Then there is no clean water to drink.

Salty seas

Most of the water in the world is salty sea water. It would make us sick if we drank it.

The salt that we put on our food is taken from the sea. In the picture below, the man is drying salt out.

The water cycle

All the water on the Earth flows in a big circle. **1** The sun heats water, turning it to gas, which rises and turns back to water droplets in the sky, making cloud. **2** As the cloud gets bigger, the water droplets join together. **3** When they get too big and heavy, they fall as rain.

Fog

What is fog?

When fine water droplets, or "vapour", hang in the air close to the ground, it is called "fog". When it's foggy, it can be hard to recognise even the places that you know well.

In the clouds

A fog is like a cloud that has sunk to the ground. Hills, mountains and other high places sometimes become covered in thick cloud. When this happens, walkers can get lost in the cloud.

Fog and smog

Smog is just what it sounds like – a smelly mixture of smoke and fog. It is often smoggy in big cities when smoke and car fumes get mixed with water droplets in the air.

Sounds and smells

People find fog annoying because we use our eyes to help us get around. But many animals don't care about fog at all. They have a keen sense of smell and good hearing, so they can find their way, whatever the weather may be!

Foggy breath

On cold days, the water in your breath turns into droplets. You can see them as a small cloud when you breathe out.

Snow

Glistening shapes

Millions of snowflakes fall when it snows. Each flake is made up of snow crystals. Each crystal has its own special pattern, so no two snowflakes are the same!

Snow clouds

When the temperature falls to freezing or below, ice crystals begin to form up in the clouds.

Soon these crystals join together and they become heavy. Then they fall as snow. Ahh!

Thirsty work

In very cold weather, it's difficult for birds to find water to drink that isn't frozen. But when it snows, they can get a drink by eating the snow.

Fun in the snow!

Some toboggans have flat bottoms which help you to travel quickly over the snow. A tray or a plastic bag works brilliantly too.

On the slopes

Many people look forward to snowy winter weather because they can go skiing.

You can learn to ski on small ski slopes and move on to bigger ones when you get better!

Very cold places

Brrr!
Our winters are mild compared to the freezing cold weather of the Arctic and Antarctic.

The animals and humans that live there have clever ways of keeping warm.

Cosy plants
Many plants living in cold areas grow in low clumps. This protects them from wind and snow.

Polar bears
A female polar bear digs a snow den, where she gives birth to one or two cubs. They stay by their mother's side for two years. Body fat and thick fur keep them warm.

Good dad

A mother emperor penguin lays an egg when winter begins. The father balances the egg on his feet and keeps it warm under a flap of skin. He stands like this until it hatches.

Creature comfort

People who live in the freezing Arctic keep warm by doing what the animals do – wrapping up in thick layers of fur!

Darkness

Day and night

Every day the Earth turns in a circle. Night begins when our part of the Earth turns away from the Sun.

Making light

In winter, it gets dark early. Years ago, people would go to bed early or use candles to see by. Now we use lights to carry on having fun into the evening!

Night lights

When it's dark, people use lights to see what they are doing. At night, we use energy stored in coal, oil and gas to heat and light our homes, to power factories and to run cars, buses and trains.

Seeing...

Night creatures, such as owls, frogs and toads, have large eyes to help them see in the dark.

Glow in the dark

If you ride your bike or go out after dark, make sure you wear reflective clothing so that other people can see you.

Reflectors help to keep you safe because the light from headlights bounces off them, making them shine, so that you can be seen in the dark.

Time zones

What time is it?

When it is daytime in Britain, it is night-time in Australia, and the other way around. What time of day it is depends on where in the world you live.

It is midday in London. Kate is eating her lunch. Look at what all her friends around the world are doing.

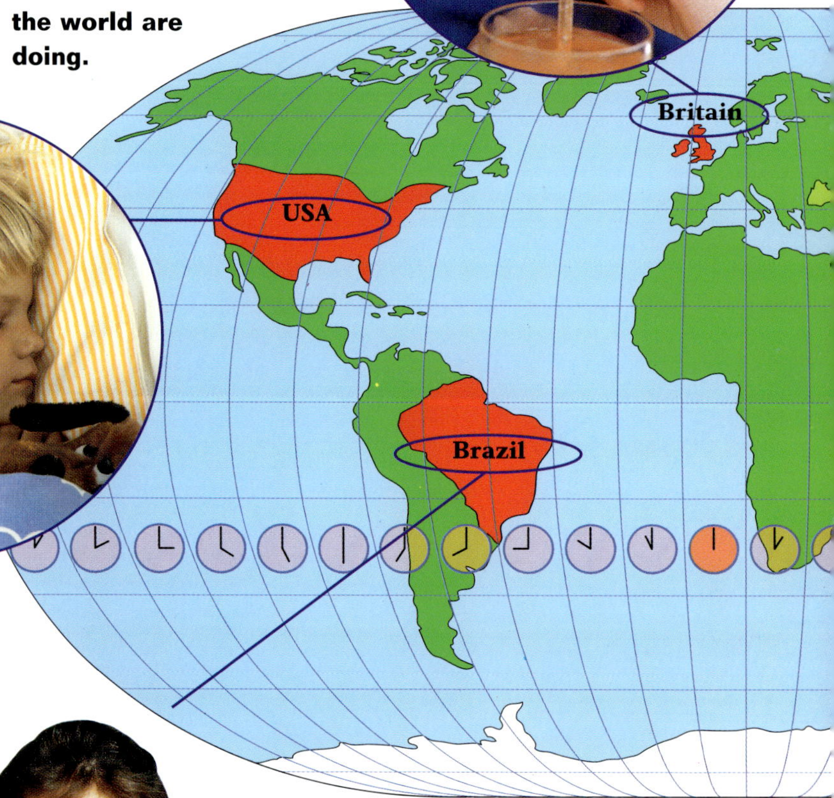

In Los Angeles, USA, it is only four o'clock in the morning and dark. Charlie is still fast asleep in bed.

Changing times

The world is divided into 24 time zones. As you move from one zone to another, time changes.

Start at 12 o'clock in London, then move around the world to see how the time changes.

In Rio de Janeiro, Brazil, Maria is going to school. It is nine o'clock in the morning.

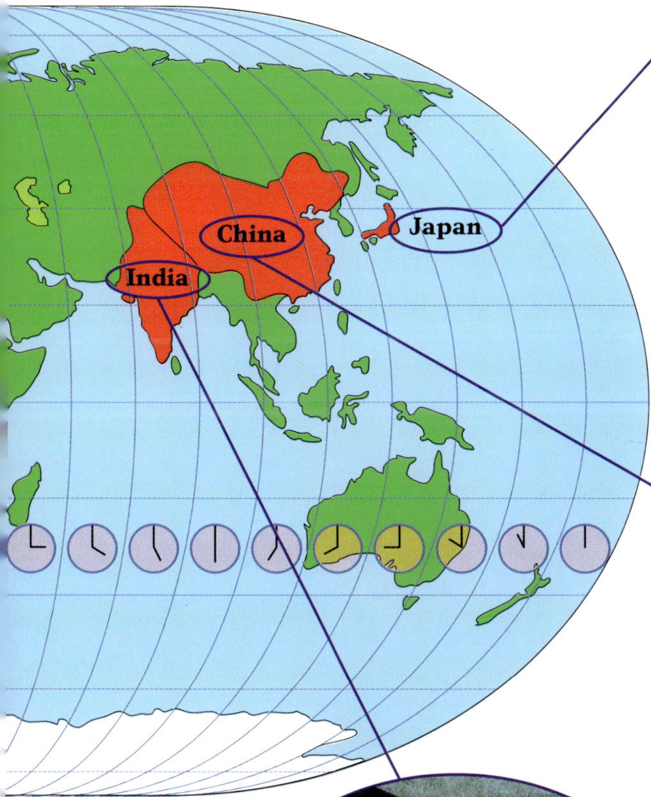

In Tokyo, Japan, it is later still. It is nine o'clock in the evening and Kazu is in bed.

In Beijing, China, it is eight o'clock in the evening. Kar-wei is eating dinner.

In New Delhi, India, it is half-past five in the afternoon and Suman and her friend are playing after school.

Hibernation

Sleep tight

In the autumn, many animals get ready to sleep all through the winter. This sleep is called "hibernation".

Dozy dormice

In autumn, animals such as hedgehogs and dormice eat lots of food and grow fat. Then they go to sleep for the winter.

They live off the fat they have stored up, so they don't need to go out to find food.

Warm for winter

In the autumn, all sorts of animals get ready to hibernate. Most people know that bears hibernate, but did you know that ladybirds do, too? They all nestle into sheltered places like sheds or under logs.

I'm so hungry...

Hedgehogs and other hibernating animals lose a lot of weight while they are asleep. When they wake up from hibernation, they're weak and very hungry. So the first thing they do is look for food.

Who's asleep?

Toads and bats spend most of the winter hibernating. Foxes and badgers stay awake, looking for food, in the winter.

Migration

Winter holiday

When the weather gets cold, some birds fly away to a warmer country. This journey is called "migration".

Home birds

Not all birds migrate to warmer places. Magpies and blackbirds stay here all winter long. They eat berries and insects.

Winter visitors

Not all birds migrate away. Some come to stay instead. Golden-eye ducks arrive in October and stay for the winter.

Butterflies flutter by

Birds are not the only creatures which migrate. Some insects also migrate in autumn. Painted Lady butterflies leave Europe for the hot deserts of Africa.

Fly away!

Watch out for big flocks of birds gathering together to fly to warmer countries.

They wait for a strong wind to start them off on their long journey.

Spot a redwing

Some birds come to Europe for the mild winter weather.

Redwings fly from very cold places. They travel at night, calling to each other in the darkness.

Midsummer

Summer stones

Midsummer has long been thought of as a magical time. We know this because of stone circles like Stonehenge in England, which was built 4,000 years ago. In England, the longest day of the year is 21st June. On that day, as the sun rises, it shines through a gap in the circle onto a special stone called the "sun stone".

Dawn chorus

Every day, birds sing just after the sun rises. At Midsummer, they might wake you up in the middle of the night!

Harvest festival

Harvest is the time of year when many of the foods we eat, like wheat for making bread and apples, are ready to pick. People have always celebrated this time because there is lots of food.

Harvest festivals

Your school or church might have a harvest festival in the autumn.

The festival reminds us that food has to be grown and be picked, and doesn't just come from supermarkets! It is a time to give thanks.

Harvest celebrations

Other countries have their own special harvest traditions too. This girl is dancing at the "good rice harvest festival" in Japan.

Bumper crops

In autumn, so much food is ready to eat that people can't always eat it all. Sometimes they save or "preserve" it to eat later in the year.

Fruits are preserved in sugar to make jam and onions and beetroot are pickled in vinegar.

Cereal harvest

Cereal crops, such as barley are usually grown in large fields. At harvest time, farmers use machines called "combine harvesters" to cut and gather the ripe crops.

Spring

Welcome spring

As winter turns to spring, the days get longer and warmer. Animals that have been sleeping through the cold months wake up, flowers bloom and birds sing!

Frogspawn

Look out for white, jelly-like balls of frogspawn in ponds. The black dot in the middle of each ball is a frog egg. These will grow into tadpoles and then into frogs!

Feathering a nest

Have you noticed the birds getting noisier? They sing songs to attract a mate.

Then the birds collect twigs, wool, feathers and straw to make a nest. This jackdaw is even getting hair from a horse's back!

Woodland flowers

Primroses and bluebells grow in woods in the spring when the sun warms up the ground.

Wake up!

Peacock butterflies sleep through the winter. They wake up when the days get longer.

Luckily, when butterflies wake up, the flowers they feed on also start to open up!

April fool!

April Fool's Day began because of cuckoos. A mother cuckoo tricks other birds into bringing up her baby for her. So on 1st April, people play tricks on each other!

Summer

Summer days

In summer, the weather is warm and the days are long. This is because the part of the Earth we live on is tilted towards the sun. The sunlight makes it warmer and lighter than in winter.

Storm warning!

Hot weather can make some amazing storms. Watch out for heavy rain, lightning and thunder on hot summer nights.

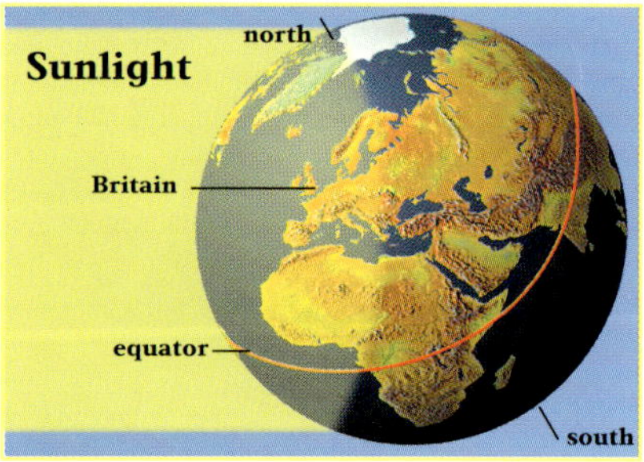

In the summer, the North Pole tilts towards the sun, making the days north of the equator longer and hotter.

City heat

Traffic gives off heat and makes cities hotter than the countryside in summer.

Also, cool air can't move easily through a city because tall buildings get in the way.

Sun safety

Always remember to wear sunscreen and a hat when you go out in the sun. Without proper protection, the hot sun can burn your skin.

Bugs for breakfast

In summer, birds like this flycatcher look for insects to feed to their babies.

Ponds and plants attract insects into your garden and the birds won't be far behind!

Autumn

All about autumn

The weather becomes colder and wetter as summer turns to autumn. As it gets cooler, the leaves turn red, yellow and brown and begin to fall from the trees.

Ripe fruit

Many fruits and berries ripen at this time of year. Can you find any rosehips like these?

Some birds love to eat rosehips, so if they spot them before you do, they'll eat the lot!

Damp display

Mushrooms and fungi like the damp autumn weather. Look out for them on trees or old tree stumps.

Sparkly spiders' webs

You can often see spiders' webs covered in dew in the autumn. Look out for them glistening on hedges and over the grass in the early morning sun.

Winter coats

When it starts to get colder in the autumn, many animals, like this fox, grow thicker fur. This keeps them warm in winter. Have any of your pets grown new winter coats?

Winter

Wrap up

Brrr! It's chilly in the winter. Remember your coat, hat and gloves if you go outside.

Chilly mist

Sometimes when it's cold, millions of water droplets collect together near the ground to make fog or mist.

Feed the birds

It's great fun going to the park on a cold day to feed the ducks and swans.

They may be hungry, but ducks don't worry about cold and wet weather! This is because their feathers are covered in waterproof oil.

Teahouse
Help the birds by feeding them when food is scarce.
Here's a simple way: push a post into the garden. Stick a loaf of bread on top. Push a pencil into it for birds to sit on when they eat the bread.

Insect antifreeze

Some butterflies and insects live through cold winters in amazing ways. There is a special chemical in their blood which stops them freezing.

They hide under dead leaves, in logs or in sheds until the spring comes.

Puffed-up feathers

In really cold weather, birds like this thrush puff up their feathers. It makes them look fatter.

The feathers trap a layer of air, just like a duvet does. This keeps the bird warm.

Saving the planet

Go green

Many things that people do, like dumping waste, are very bad for the environment. But there's a lot we can do to look after our world and make it a cleaner place. Here's how...

On your bike!

Cycling or walking keeps you fit and is great fun – and it doesn't use any fuel except your energy! So use your bike whenever you can, especially on short journeys.

Try walking to school or share the car journey with a friend. Fewer cars on the road mean less damage to the air.

Hedge home

Lots of wildlife lives in hedges. But in the last 50 years many hedgerows have been dug up. Now people are replanting them, making new homes for animals.

Sea damage

Even huge oceans can be polluted by people. In 1999, an oil tanker spilled 10,000 tonnes of oil near France, killing birds and other sea life.

People power

Recycling our rubbish, like paper and bottles, helps to protect the environment and saves energy. If you take 20 cans to a recycling bin, you will save enough electricity to run your television for an hour.